華藝 II
Oriental Flower Arrangement II

華藝 II

Oriental Flower Arrangement II

任 華公 著　Im Wha Kong

華藝 II
1984年 3 月＊第 1 刷發行

著者＊任華公
寫眞＊主婦の友社
取材協力＊大韓民國文化公報部
發行者＊石川晴彦
發行處＊主婦の友社
　　　　〒101 日本國東京都千代田區神田駿河台 1 － 6
　　　　電話　東京(03)294－1111
社團法人華公會＊〒110 大韓民國서울特別市鍾路區通義洞10
　　　　電話（서울）723－6305

First printing, 1984

Published by SHUFUNOTOMO CO., LTD.
1-6, Kanda Surugadai, Chiyoda-ku, Tokyo, 101 Japan

Wha Kong Hoe Corporation:
(Im Wha Kong Flower Arrangement Society)
10, Tongui-dong, Jongro-ku, Seoul, Korea
Tel: (seoul) 723-6305

Printed in Japan　　　　　　　　ISBN　4-07-973116-X

前 文

世界의 꽃친구들에게

　華芸 I 에 이어 다시 華芸 II 를 내게 되어 기쁩니다.
　꽃을 通하여 많은 친구들과 풍부한 경험을 얻게되었고, 이 모든것들
이 이 책을 내는 밑거름이 되었읍니다.

　華芸 II 는 華芸 I 에서 다루어지지 않았던 部分을 수록하고 一部는 東
洋의 건축과 自然을 背景으로 하였읍니다.

　이 冊을 出版하는데 도움을 주신 文化公報部와 主婦之友社에 深深한
감사를 드립니다.

　이 冊이 東洋을 사랑하고 東洋의 꽃을 理解하는데, 조그만　보탬이
되기를 간절히 바라는 바입니다.

任華公

Preface

to my friends, the friends of flowers everywhere in the world

It is a great pleasure to see the publication of Whaye (Oriental Flower Arrangement) II. Through the beautiful medium of flowers, I have gained many friends and many rich experiences which have provided me with constant inspiration in the writing of this book.

The many days and years I have spent with flowers have brought me endless enjoyment. I hope that Whaye II, by supplementing Whaye I, will bring to you, dear friend, the happiness and peace of mind that flowers can give. Besides dealing with the principles of flower arrangement, I have also tried to deal with the structure and background of oriental aesthetics and with the influence of nature on it.

I wish to express my deep gratitude to the Department of Public Relations of the Republic of Korea and to Shufunotomo Co., Ltd. for their interest and cooperation without which this book would not have been possible.

If in only a small way Whaye II serves to instill a love for the Orient and an understanding on Oriental Flower Arrangement, I shall feel that my life's work has been rewarded.

Jm. Wha Kong

目　次

Contents

華　藝

　　아름다운 것은 東西古今을 通하여 아름답습니다.

　　또 아름다움에의 동경은 自然으로 向한 사랑으로 表現되어, 先人들의 心中에 깃들었던, 美에 對한 추구가 여러 가지 형태로 오늘을 生活하는 우리에게 흐르고 있읍니다.

　　自然을 사랑하며 自然에 順應 하면서 陰陽의 原理를 의심치 않고 生活한 東洋사람들에게 있어서 自然은 존엄하고 그리고 한없이 아름다운 것이었읍니다.

　　깊은 겨울을 넘긴 梅花 봉오리에서 生命의 환희를 느끼고 草木의 自然에서 出生의 존엄을 지켜 보았읍니다.

　　꽃은 生命이 있다는 것을 잊어서는 안됩니다. 살아있는 꽃은 항상 變합니다. 꽃과 꽃봉오리는 형태가 다를 뿐 아니라 살아있는 것에 時間을 느끼게 합니다. 꽃을 오래 지키는 努力도 技術과 더불어 필요 합니다.

　　꽃의 自然感이나 꽃의 個性을 각기 適切하게 表現하는 것도 重要하고, 構成에 있어서 리듬, 均衡, 運動感, 量感, 色彩와 質感 等等 여러가지 기술적인 연구와 修業은 꽃을 工夫하는 사람들에게 주어진 즐거운 과제입니다.

　　華藝는 어김없이 三枝法에 의해 구성되고 空間의 아름다움과 더불어 强弱, 疎密의 度를 생각하고, 꽃에서 精神的인 德性을 인정하고 있읍니다.

　　自然을 向한 아름다움을 짙게 가꾸는 東洋의 華藝는 오랜 歷史속에서 피어난 東洋人의 花心을 모든 사람들에게 그지없이 전하리라 믿습니다.

　　꽃을 사랑하는 마음과 誠意있는 준비와 끝없는 修鍊은 좋은 꽃을 꽂을 수 있는 條件이라고 믿어 마지 않습니다.

Whaye—The Art of Flowers

Beauty is never-changing. It knows no limits of time nor boundaries between peoples. Through the ages the longing human beings have for beauty has sprung from love for the wonders of nature's own creation. This longing has found expression in the arts, customs, and philosophies that have been handed down to us today.

The Oriental, who loved nature and based life upon the ying-yang laws of nature, revered the natural world for its absolute beauty. The joy of life was felt in the budding branches of the apricot tree which braves the cold of winter bloom even in the snow. In the birth and rebirth of the grasses of the field was felt the loneliness of life.

Being alive, flowers must change. This obvious but often overlooked truth must always be kept in mind. A bud and a full-blown flower differ not only in appearance, they also convey different impressions of time, for the one is filled with expectation while the other has already reached its prime. To keep flowers alive therefore requires both skill and care.

It is also important to portray the natural tendencies and individual attributes of a flower. Achieving this presents a fascinating opportunity to study the techniques used to bring rhythm, balance, movement, color, form, and character into a composition.

The art of arranging flowers is based unfailingly on the Rule of Three, which, by observing the beauty of empty space and the contrasts of strong and weak, full and sparse, enlivens the spirit of each flower.

Cultivating an aesthetic close to nature, the people of the orient have created a long history of flower arranging. My deepest wish is to convey this love of flowers to every corner of the earth. I ask only that those who follow this path have a true love for flowers and that they pursue their study with a sincere and patient heart.

歴史와 꽃들

Flowers and the Orient

景福宮, 塔
Kyongbokkung Palace

花器　白磁円筒花瓶
素材　山歸來, 유－까리, 맨드라미, 古木
Container: White porcelain cylindrical vase
Materials: Green brier, Eucalyptus, Cockscomb, Aged tree

景福宮, 慶會樓
Kyongbokkung Palace
Kyonghoeru Pavilion

花器　白磁瓶
素材　黄菊花, 石榴, 古木
Container: White porcelain
　　　　　 vase with narrow
　　　　　 neck
Materials: Chrysanthemum,
　　　　　 Pomegranate,
　　　　　 Aged tree

11

花器　白磁水盤
素材　白菊花，鶏頭花，버섯
Container: White porcelain water basin
Materials: Chrysanthemum, Cockscomb, Hoelen mushrooms

花器　白磁八角瓶
素材　소나무，黃薔薇
Container: White porcelain octagonal vase
Materials: Pine, Rose

景福宮，勤政殿
Kunjongjon Hall

13

花器　白磁鉢
素材　글라디올러스
Container: White porcelain bowl
Material: Gladiolus

昌德宮，仁政殿
Changdokkung Palace
Injongjon Hall

花器　白磁水盤
素材　코스모스, 밤
Container: White porcelain water basin
Materials: Cosmos, Chestnut

昌德宮, 금천교
Kumchonkyo Bridge

花器　오지자배기
素材　감, 피마자, 朱木, 땅두릅, 古木(은행나무 뿌리)
Container: Deep bowl for pickled kimchi
Materials: Persimmon, Castor-oil plant, Flower of udo salad (Aralia Cordata),
　　　　　Aged root of gingko, Yew (taxus cuspidata)

花器　白磁水盤
素材　菖蒲, 映山紅, 沈至梅
Container: White porcelain water basin
Materials: Japanese iris, Azalea, False-spiraea

코리아 하우스
Korea Hause

花器　新羅土器
素材　梧桐씨, 梧桐꽃몽우리,
　　　　시크라멘
Container: Silla ware vase
Materials: Buds and fruits of
　　　　paulownia, Cyclamen

花器　白磁花瓶
素材　山歸來, 石榴, 白菊花, 小菊花
Container: White porcelain basin
Materials: Green brier, Pomegranate,
　　　　Chrysanthemum

慶州, 三体石佛
Triple Buddhas, Kyongiu

花器　白磁大壺
素材　洋蘭，スプリンゲリアスパラガス，ミリオグラダスアスパラガス
Container: Large white porcelain vase
Materials: Phalaenopsis, Dendrobium phalaenopsis, Cymbidium, Asparagus myriocladus, Driftwood

金谷陵
Kumgoknung Tombs; Kings of Korea, Kojong and Sunjong

21

花器　白磁花瓶
素材　소나무, 洋蘭, 南天씨, 古木
Container: White porcelain tall vase
Materials: Pine, Cattleya, Nandina, Driftwood

金谷陵
Kumgoknung Tombs, Statue of Civil

22

自然의 꽃들
Creative Work

花器　白磁花瓶
素材　소나무, 梅花, 薔薇, 古木
Container: White porcelain vase
Materials: Pine, Japanese apricot, Rose, Aged tree

花器　白磁鉢
素材　버들강아지, 冬栢
Container: White porcelain bowl
Materials: Pussy willow, Camellia

花器　白磁鉢
素材　소나무, 梅花, 冬栢, 古木
Container: White porcelain bowl
Materials: Pine, Japanese apricot, Camellia, Aged tree

花器　白磁水盤
素材　진달래, 둥굴레, 迎春花, 기우이덩굴, 古木
Container: White porcelain water basin
Materials: Azalea, Solomon's-seal, Winter sweet, Vine of kiwi fruits, Aged tree

28

花器　白磁鉢
素材　개나리, 유채화
Container: White porcelain bowl
Materials: Weeping forsythia, Rape blossom stalk

花器　白磁鉢
素材　박달나무, 라낭큘러스, 古木, 미리오글라다스아스파라거스
Container:　White porcelain bowl
Materials:　Giant dogwood, Ranunculus, Asparagus myriocladus, Aged tree

花器　白磁花瓶
素材　물싸리꽃, 아네모네, 木蓮가지
Container: White porcelain vase
Materials: Spirea thumbergii, Anemone, Branch of lily magnolia

花器　白磁水盤
素材　紫木蓮, 푸른단풍, 아이리스, 古木, 마른가지
Container: White porcelain water basin
Materials: Lily magnolia, Fullmoon maple, Iris, Aged tree, Dried branch

花器　白磁花瓶
素材　紫木蓮，芍薬，古木
Container: White porcelain vase
Materials: Lily magnolia, Chinese peony, Aged tree

花器　白磁大鉢
素材　박달나무꽃, 芍薬, 古木
Container: White porcelain large bowl
Materials: Giant dogwood, Chinese peony, Aged tree, Driftwood

34

花器　유리花瓶
素材　등꽃, 芍藥
Container: Glass vase
Materials: Wisteria, Chinese peony

花器　白磁鉢
素材　爻菖蒲，映山紅
Container: White porcelain bowl
Materials: Japanese iris, Azalea

花器　白磁酒瓶
素材　물싸리가지, 수국꽃
Container: White porcelain wine bottle
Materials: Branch of spirea thumbergii, Hydrangea

花器　白磁花瓶
素材　百合，觀賞用사과，아가판사스，古木
Container: White porcelain vase
Materials: Korean lily, Apple tree, Agapanthas, Aged tree

花器　白磁鉢
素材　가－베라，스모－크츄리－
Container: White porcelain bowl
Materials: Transvaal daisy, Smoke tree

花器　白磁鉢
素材　패랭이꽃, 스위트살탄, 베이비브
　　　레스, 용수초
Container: White porcelain bowl
Material:　Japanese spirea, Sweet sultan,
　　　　　Baby's breath, Bulrush

花器　木器花瓶
素材　山歸來, 薔薇
Container: Wooden vase
Materials:　Green brier, Rose

花器　白磁八角瓶
素材　알륨, 아가판사스, 沈至梅, 메리－아스
　　　파라거스
Container: White porcelain octagonal vase
Materials: Allium giganteum, Agapanthas,
　　　　　　False-spirea, Asparagus merry

花器　大理石콤포－트
素材　映山紅, 베이비브레스
Container: Marble compote
Materials: Azalea, Baby's breath

花器　白磁水盤
素材　睡蓮
Container: White porcelain water basin
Material:　Water lily

花器　白磁小鉢
素材　용담초, 물싸리
Container: White porcelain bowl
Materials: Gentian, Twig of spirea thumbergii

花器　白磁鉢
素材　스타 - 치스카스피아, 제라늄
Container: White porcelain bowl
Materials: Statice Caspia, Geranium

花器 이태리유리花器
素材 크리마티스
Container: Italian glass vase
Material: Clematis

花器　이태리유리花器
素材　山歸來, 해바라기, 크리마티스, 黄色칼라릴리
Container: Italian glass vase
Materials: Green brier, Sun flower, Clematis, Calla lily

花器　白磁鉢
素材　마타리,　억새풀,　수리취,　쇼－위리리,　鶏頭花
Container: White porcelain bowl
Materials: Patrinia scabiosaefolia, Chinese miscanthus, Blue ball, Variegated lily, Cockscomb

花器　白磁花瓶
素材　섬으름, 마타리, 山나리, 古木
Container: White porcelain vase
Materials: Stauntonia, Patrinia scabiosaefolia, Starlily, Aged tree, Dried branch

花器　白磁花瓶
素材　코스모스, 미리오글라다스아스파라거스
Container: White porcelain vase with narrow neck
Materials: Cosmos, Asparagus myriocladus

48

花器　白磁콤포-트
素材　黃色글라디올러스, 페레-지, 부들
Container: White porcelain compote
Materials: Gladiolus, Great cattail, Statice perezii

49

花器　촛병
素材　유채화, 古木
Container: Vinegar pot
Materials: Rape blossoms, Driftwood

花器　白磁酒瓶
素材　스위트피-, 란잎
Container: White porcelain wine bottle
Materials: Sweet pea, Orchid leaves

花器　白磁酒瓶
素材　薔薇
Container: White porcelain wine bottle
Material:　Rose

花器　陶器花瓶
素材　마타리, 黄色나리
Container: Bizen-yaki vase
Materials: Patrinia scabiosaefolia, Lily

花器　제주도木器 二点
素材　밤송이, 도라지, 크리마티스, 강아지풀
Containers: Two wooden containers from Cheju-do Island
Materials:　Chestnut, Chinese bell flower, Clematis, Fox tail

花器　白磁酒瓶
素材　스프레이菊花, 은단초
Container: White porcelain wine bottle
Materials: Spraymum, Japanese beauty berry

花器　青磁鉢
素材　다알리아, 葉蘭, 표백뽕나무
Container: Celadon porcelain bowl
Materials: Dahlia, Aspidistra, Bleached common broom

花器　멕시코花器
素材　뿔가지, 洋蘭
Container: Mexican Pot
Materials: Fox-face, Orchid (epidendrum)

花器　멕시코花器
素材　후리-지야, 冬栢
Container: Mexican Pot
Materials: Freesia, Camellia

花器　白磁花瓶
素材　단풍, 까치밥열매, 菊花, 古木
Container: White porcelain vase
Materials: Crimson Japanese maple, Bittersweet, Chrysanthemum, Aged tree

花器　白磁鉢
素材　단풍, 까치밥열매, 菊花
Container: White porcelain bowl
Materials: Crimson Japanese maple, Bittersweet, Small chrysanthemum

花器　青色花瓶
素材　白木蓮, 버들강아지, 스토크, 아룸, 메리아스파라거스　古木
Containers:　Korean blue vases
Materials:　Yulan, Pussy willow, Gilly flower, Allium, Asparagus merry, Driftwood

꽃이야기

Techniques

白磁花器　White Porcelain Containers

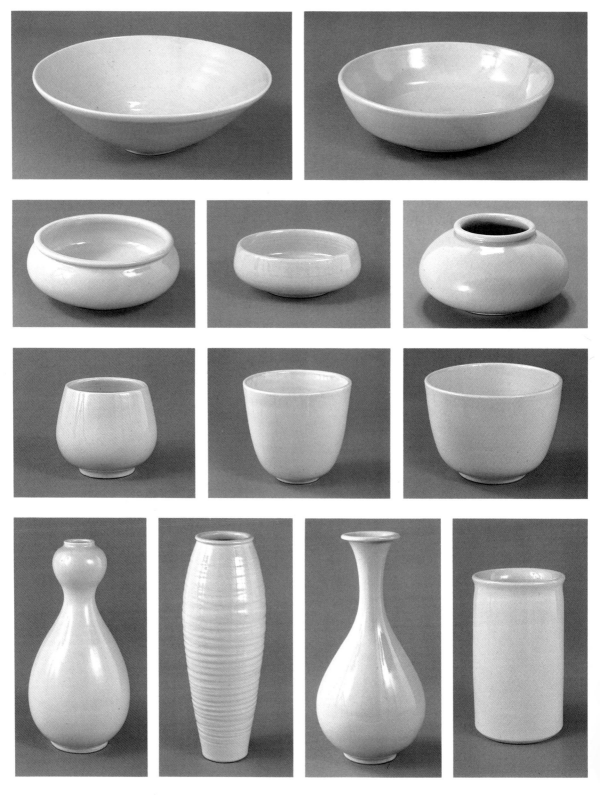

著者가 디자인한 花器들과 가마
Designed by the author

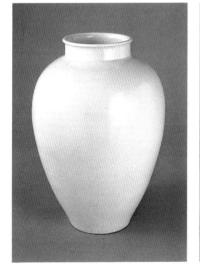

63

素材의 선택과 배합

우선 素材를 선택할 경우 꽂는 목적, 환경, 사용할 수 있는 花器를 생각하고 꽂는 사람이 表現하고자 하는 意図가 反映되어 정해 진다.

모든 素材에는 季節感 외에 色彩, 形態, 質感 量感 등 構成上의 要素를 考慮한다는 것은 重要한 일이지만 文学的 歷史的 또는 風習에 의한 꽃에의 이미지가 꽃을 선택하고 배합하는데 매우 중요한 일이다.

季節感을 강조하고 싶을 때는 같은 季節의 植物을 配合하는 것이 一般的이지만 때로는 마른 나무, 着色한 素材, 古木 등을 配合하여 素材의 季節感을 한층 더하게 한다.

形態上의 대조적인 配合도 一般的으로 많이 쓰이고 있다.

카네이션과 아스파라거스의 配合은 代表的인 形態와 色의 대조적인 配合이다.

무엇과 무엇을 配合하는가는 時期와 내용에 따라 季節을 重要視할 것인가, 行事의 主題에 重点을 둘 것인가, 아니면 다만 色相, 形態, 質, 量感에 따라 꽂는 사람의 表現에 重点을 둘 것인가에 따라 결정된다.

技法에 따라서는 温室栽培에 의해서 나도는 각기 다른 季節의 꽃도 한 花器안에 消化할 수가 있다.

봄에 싹튼 버들가지와 가을꽃인 温室栽培의 국화를 配合하였을 때도 非写実的 処理에 의해 버들가지의 선과 국화의 빛깔과 덩어리로 사용할 수가 있다. 線과 덩어리의 대조적인 사용방법으로 季節感覚을 抹殺하는 手法이다.

베이비브레스와 장미는 点과 덩어리
소나무와 장미는 質感, 線과 덩어리

설날이나 크리스마스에 소나무, 전나무, 장미 포인세치아 등은 因習에 의한 꽃의 配合이라고 할 수 있을 것이다.

하나의 花器속에 꽂는 素材를 한가지類로 하느냐 두가지 세가지 많은 素材를 配合하는 가는 각자의 기호이며 특별한 규정은 없다.

카ー라리리 한가지만으로 꽂아도 하얀 꽃과 뚜렷한 줄기의 선과 넓은 面을 가진 잎은 각기 대조적인 色彩, 形態와 質感으로 각기 다른 要素가 調和되어 그 対比가 또 아름다움을 낳게 하는 것이다.

素材의 빛깔, 形態, 質感, 線(直線과 曲線) 크기, 季節感 또는 運動感과 重点, 方向性 등 素材가 갖는 特性을 잘 아는 素材에 대한 지식은 보다 나은 배합을 할 수가 있으며 作品에 変化를 주고 아름다운 조화를 이룰 수 있다.

꽃이 사람들의 마음에 어떻게 비치는가 하는 것은 꽃 自体의 아름다움 뿐아니라 그 꽃이 피는 季節과 그 꽃이 있는 環境 그리고 文学的背景 歷史的 背景도 포함된다.

配合을 할 때에도 이런일들을 마음에 두어야 한다.

The Choosing and Combining of Materials

If you would like to emphasize a seasonal feeling it is best to choose only those plants that appear in the particular season you wish to portray. Occasionally, however, you may find that dried and colored materials or aged branches make an interesting contrast and thus enhance the mood of that season.

The combination of contrasting materials is a fundamental technique. A typical contrasting combination in terms of both color and shape is carnation and asparagus. The contrast can be based on season, on mood and character, or on physical attributes such as color, shape, texture, or size. If done properly, it is possible, for instance, to take flowers of different seasons that have been grown in a greenhouse. One may arrange spring-like pussywillow with chrysanthemums, which are fall flowers, in order to make imaginative use of the willow's flowing lines as opposed to the chrysanthemum's solid mass of color.

A composition of dots and mass is achieved with baby's breath and rose. Contrast in character, line and mass is brought about by combining a pine branch with roses.

Traditional combinations for Christmas and the New Year holidays are also examples of contrast: pine (line, green), fir (mass, green), rose and poinsettia (mass, red), lily (line, white).

Whether to make a mono-material or a poly-material arrangement is a decision that lies entirely with the individual. No rules exist. Even if you work solely with calla lily, for instance, you still will have plenty of contrast in color, shape, and texture with its white flowers and the sharp lines of its stems and large, flat leaves. The various beautiful elements of the plant will combine naturally to form a composition in harmony and contrast.

Above all, it is important to know your materials so that you can take full advantage of their unique characteristics. To have variety and harmony you must think of color, shape, line, texture, size, character, movement, and season. The basic principle consists of setting the strong with the weak, the high with the low, the large with the small, the hard with the soft, the bold with the delicate, and so on.

In the final analysis flowers and other materials should be selected not only for their own beauty, but also for the effect they will have on the viewer's feelings.

三枝法　The Rule of Three

三枝法에 의한 基本花型

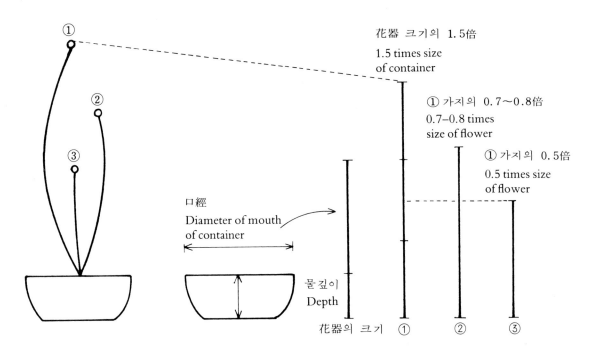

花器 크기의 1.5倍
1.5 times size
of container

① 가지의 0.7～0.8倍
0.7-0.8 times
size of flower

① 가지의 0.5倍
0.5 times
of flower

口經
Diameter of mouth
of container

물깊이
Depth

花器의 크기

素材에 따라 流動하는 가지의 크기
Height of Stems in a Basin

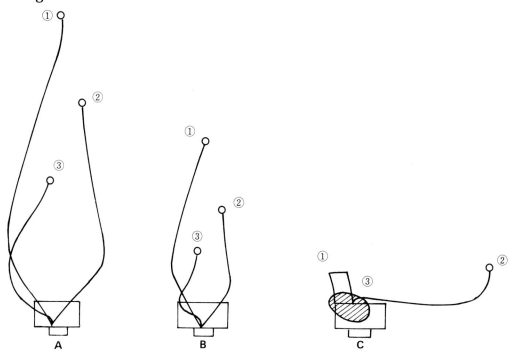

A

B

C

A : 버들가지와 같이 가늘고 긴 素材는 基本花型의 3倍 까지 높일 수 있다.

B : 카-네이션 같은 素材는 거의 基本型 대로의 크기로 安定感을 얻을 수 있다.

C : 소나무 등은 質感과 굵기에 따라 얕게 앉혀 진다.

A: Long, slender stems such as willow can be three times the usual height.

B: Flowers like carnations produce a stable impression when cut to the rules of proportion.

C: Pine branches and the like, because of their thick, heavy image, should be kept low.

直立型의 보탬가지와 針筆위 가지의 位置
Height of Stems According to Type of Material

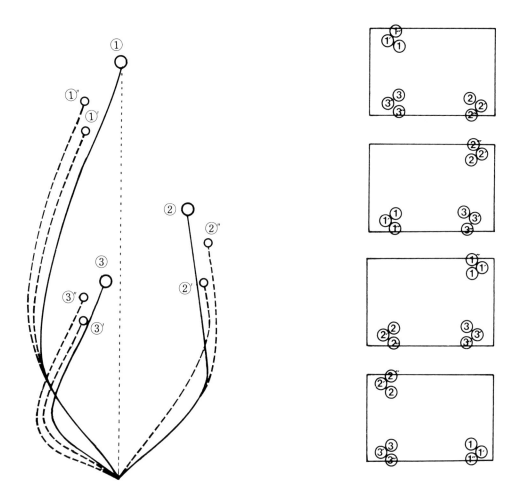

꽃의 얼굴 Angle of Pose

薔薇 Roses

서 있는 植物의 모습은 側面에서 보았을 때 가
장 分明히 그 線을 볼 수 있다.

素材를 세웠을 경우 前面, 後面에서는 그 素
材가 가지고 있는 線을 볼 수 없다.

1. 前面에서 본것
2. 側面에서 본것
3. 後面에서 본것
4. 꽃이 위로 向한것　(뉘었을때)
5. 꽃이 아래로 向한것 (　〃　)

The line of an upright plant is most impres-
sive when seen in profile. Viewed from the front
or back, the line loses its personality.

1: and 2: Front, side, and 3: Rear poses
4: Flower facing up when slanted
5: Flower facing down when slanted

튜-립 Tulips

　튜-립같이 모양이 單純하고 잎의 수가 적은 植物은 꽃과 잎의 간격이나 잎의 달리는 모습을 잘 보아서 꽃과 잎, 줄기의 균형이 잡히도록 한다.

1. 前面에서 본것
2. 側面에서 본것
3. 後面에서 본것
4. 꽃이 위로 向한것　（뉘었을때）
5. 꽃이 아래로 向한것（　〃　）

　Plants like tulips that have a simple shape and few leaves, require attention to the overall balance of the flowers, leaves, and stems. An arrangement based on the way they naturally grow is best-suited for such materials.

1: and 2: Front, side, and 3: Rear poses
4: Flower facing up when slanted
5: Flower facing down when slanted

데포딜 **Daffodils**

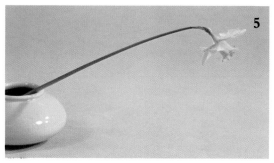

水仙이나 해바라기같이 꽃의 얼굴이 分明한 꽃은 옆에서 보았을 때는 줄기의 線이 아름답 지만 꽃의 强한 表情은 잡을 수가 없다.

1. 前面에서 본것
2. 側面에서 본것
3. 後面에서 본것
4. 꽃이 위로 向한것　(뉘었을때)
5. 꽃이 아래로 向한것　(　〃　)

The stem of daffodils and sunflowers and other flowers that have a definite frontal face looks especially beautiful viewed from the side. In this case, however, it becomes difficult to catch the strong expression of the flowers themselves.

1: and 2: Front, side, and 3: Rear poses
4: Flower facing up when slanted
5: Flower facing down when slanted

카네이션 **Carnations**

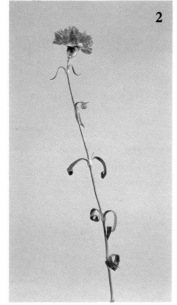

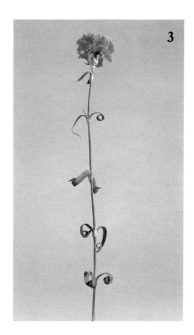

꽃을 기울여서 낮게 꽂을 때 꽃을 먼저 세운
다.

이때 만약 꽃을 앞으로 向해 세워서 기울이
면 꽃얼굴은 아래로 向한다.

꽃은 後面이 보이도록 세운 다음 누르면서 기
울이면 꽃얼굴은 위로 向하게 되여 마치 太陽아
래서 피었을때와 같은 表情이 된다.

1. 前面에서 본것
2. 側面에서 본것
3. 後面에서 본것
4. 꽃이 위로 向한것 　(뉘었을때)
5. 꽃이 아래로 向한것 　(〃)

Carnations in a low, leaning arrangement
are first inserted vertically and then are
slanted. If the flower faces front when inserted,
it will face downward after being slanted. For
this reason, it should first be placed into the
container facing towards the back. This will
cause it to face skyward when it is pushed over,
just as it would do in the sunshine.

1: and 2: Front, side, and 3: Rear poses
4: Flower facing up when slanted
5: Flower facing down when slanted

국화 **Chrysanthemums**

국화, 장미같은 꽃들은 잎을 떼어서 줄기를 선명하게 보일 때가 있다.

꽃 바로 밑의 잎은 따내지 않고 남겨 놓는 것이 꽃을 풍성하고 아름답게 보이게 한다.

1. 前面에서 본것
2. 側面에서 본것
3. 後面에서 본것
4. 꽃이 위로 向한것　(뉘었을때)
5. 꽃이 아래로 向한것　(　〃　)

Trimming the leaves of roses and chrysanthemums will bring out the line of the stem and lighten the arrangement, but the leaves just below the flowers should be kept to enhance their beauty by giving them volume.

1: and 2: Front, side, and 3: Rear poses
4: Flower facing up when slanted
5: Flower facing down when slanted

72

아스페레늄 **Japanese Bird's Nest**

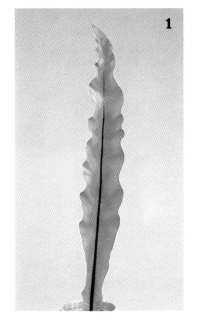

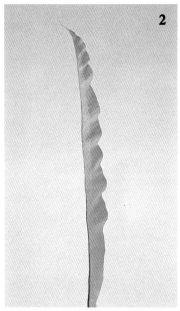

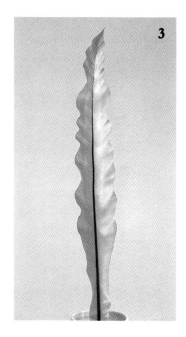

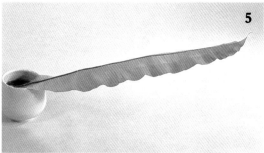

植物의 表裏나 正面, 側面, 後面은 꽃 뿐만은 아니다.

모든 植物의 꽃, 잎, 줄기, 덩굴, 열매까지도 太陽아래서 자랄 때 前面과 後面이 分明하기 때문에 꽂을 때 識別하여 처리하여야 한다.

1. 前面에서 본것
2. 側面에서 본것
3. 後面에서 본것
4. 잎面이 위로 向한것　(뉘었을때)
5. 잎面이 아래로 向한것　(　〃　)

Not only flowers, but all plants have a face, a front and back, and a profile. Leaves, flowers, stems, trunks, berries and vines—all things that grow under the sun are endowed with a front and a back. In any arrangement special care should be taken to preserve this natural phenomenom.

1: and 2: Front, side, and 3: Rear poses
4: Flower facing up when slanted
5: Flower facing down when slanted

花器　크리스탈 花瓶
素材　거-베라,
　　　미리오그라다스아스파라거스

Container: Crystal vase
Materials: Transvaal daisy, Asparagus myriocladus

74

花器　크리스탈花瓶　　Container: Crystal Vase
素材　洋蘭, 페레-지　Materials: Orchid (Phalaenopsis), Statice Perezii

투명한 花瓶에 固定 시키는 方法　Using a Transparent Container

투명한 화병을 사용할 때는 素材를 고정시킨 다음에 화병속의 素材部分이 連結되어서 투시된다는 것을 잊어서는 안된다.

① 보조가지는 꽂는 素材와 같은 것으로 한다.
② 눈에 띄는 끈으로 묶는 것을 피한다.
③ 잎, 그밖에 지저분한 것들을 정리하여 투시되는 부분을 깨끗하게 한다.

Because a transparent container reveals the lower stems that would otherwise be hidden from view, the following precautions should be taken.

1. Make supports out of the same material as the major element in the arrangement.
2. Avoid tying with conspicuous strings.
3. Trim all leaves below the surface of the water for a clean, tidy look.

75

直立型 **Upright Style**

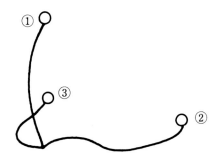

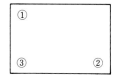

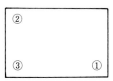

花器　白磁水盤
素材　물싸리, 薔薇

　素材가 서있을 때 모습, 옆으로 뻗은 線 그리고 面이나 덩어리의 아름다움을 가장 잘 나타낼 수 있는 花型이다.

　初心者가 基本花型을 實習하는 過程에서 쉽고 편하게 시작할 수 있는 花型이기도 하다.

Container: White porcelain basin
Materials: Spirea, Rose

　The easiest form for beginners, the upright style is suitable for combining flat or mass forms with plants that have vertical as well as horizontal lines.

下垂型 Cascade Style

花器 白磁花瓶
素材 山歸來, 노랑나리, 도라지꽃

素材의 운치를 表現하는데 適當한 花型이다.

늘어지는 덩굴, 自然스럽게 떨어지는 가지,
또는 아스파라거스와 같이 흐르는 線을 갖인 잎
等 下垂型에 쓰이는 素材는 多樣하다.

水盤에 꽂을 때는 花台위에 놓는 것이 보기
에 편하다.

높은 花瓶에 꽂았을 때 더 한층 下垂의 效果
가 强하게 表現된다.

Container: White porcelain vase
Materials: Green brier, Chinese bell flower

To express elegance there is no better
medium than the cascade style. Numerous
materials lend themselves to this style: vines,
naturally drooping branches, asparagus
branchlets. An arrangement in a basin should
be put on a pedestal to give space for the
cascading elements. A tall container is therefore all the more effective.

平面型　Flat Style

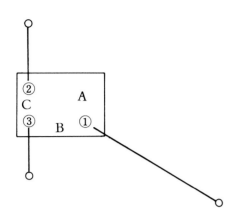

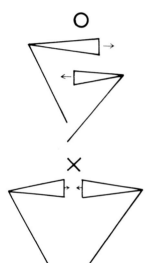

花器　白磁水盤
素材　百合哭, 薔薇

Container: White porcelain water basin
Materials: Easter lily, Rose

百合꽃은 한줄기에 두개, 세개, 때로 네개 까지도 꽃이 핀다.

꽃方向이 각기 다르게 붙어 있는 것도 百合의 특징이다.

핀 꽃의 얼굴이 正面으로 向했을 때 너무 强한 느낌을 주고 꽃方向이 左右로 놓였을 때 부드럽게 처리된다.

꽃혀진 百合꽃들은 높이를 달리 하고 각기 꽃의 方向의 延長点에서도 맞닿지 않는 것이 百合꽃을 아름답게 처리하는 요령이다.

Lilies characteristically have two or three, sometimes even four, flowers on a stem. If the stem is so placed that the fully opened flower faces front, the buds which are behind it will end up facing the rear. To avoid this, the stem should be turned, putting the opened flower in profile.

Any flower placed so that it directly faces the viewer will look stiff. Turning the flower slightly to the right or left will soften the impression and give it a more expressive viewing angle.

To make a successful arrangement with lilies, it is necessary to vary their heights, in this way eliminating awkward collisions among the flowers.

分離型 Separate Style

花器　白色유리水盤
素材　리아도리스, 薔薇

　한 花器 안에 素材를 둘로 나누어 고정시키는
花型을 分離型이라고 한다.
　투명한 花器 속에 針峯을 사용할 경우에는 푸
른 잎으로 針峯을 싸서 針峯의 금속성을 가리
워 준다.

Container: Glass flower container
Materials: Liatris, Rose

　The separate style is composed of two
independent but complementary arrangements
within the same container. If a transparent
container is used, wrap the frog in green leaves
to camouflage the metal.

花器　白磁八角瓶
素材　카네이션, 미리오그라다스아스파라거스
Container: White porcelain octagonal vase
Materials: Carnation, Asparagus Myriocladus

덩어리 Mass

元来 꽃모습이 덩어리로 되어있는 素材도 있고 덩어리로 묶어서 볼륨에 의해 아름다움을 보여 주는 素材도 있다.

수국, 맨드라미, 라일락 등은 前者이고 스위트피이 카네이션 등은 後者이다.

덩어리진 素材는 꽃뿐만 아니고 억새같은 素材 잎종류 열매 등 다양하며 여러가지 마른 素材도 묶어서 量感을 보이기 위해 쓰여지고 있다.

여기서는 스위트피이 라일락으로 볼륨을 보이고 후리지아 잎의 흐르는 선을 대조적으로 썼다.

한편 덩어리진 베이비브레스의 부드러운 흰 点의 집단을 같이 하므로서 작약의 꽃덩어리를 돋보이게 했다.

There are several kinds of plants whose flowers naturally grow in a mass such as hydrangea, cockscomb, and tree peony. There are also certain flowers that appear attractive in a mass arrangement. Examples of these include sweet peas and carnations.

Such materials as pampas grass and dried leaves or berries also can be effectively given a feeling of volume by arranging them in a mass.

Here in one arrangement volume has been created with sweet peas and white lilac, the freesia adding a flowing line. In the other example, the mass of peonies has been contrasted with the delicate white dots of baby's breath.

花器　남색유리花器
素材　후리－지아, 라일락, 스위트피－

Container: Glass container
Materials: Freesia, White lilac,
Sweet pea

花器　白磁筆筒
素材　芍藥, 베이비브레스

Container: White porcelain vase
Materials: Double peony, Baby's breath

花器　白磁花器
素材　薔薇, 오동추덩굴
Container: White porcelain bowl
Materials: Rose, Red vine

線의 움직임 Line Movement

　모든 素材의 線은 각기 다른 表情과　리듬을
갖고 있다.
　그리고 線의 흐르는 方向과 움직임에 따라 作
品의 變化는 다양하고 미묘하다.
　作例 右는 曲線을 살려서 스프레이 菊花로 매
듭을 지었다.
　作例 左는 덩굴을 平行으로 기우려서 움직임
을 보다 더 강조한 것이다.

　　All materials have a line that is unique in
feeling and rhythm. The direction and movement of that line give rise to various subtle
changes in a composition. The robust curve of
the vine in the right-hand example has been set
against the colorful spray mums. The vine in
the left-hand arrangement displays a lively
rhythm as it dances across its airy stage.

花器　오닉스花器 (멕시코)
素材　스프레이국화, 野生덩굴,
　　　스프링게리 아스파라거스
Container: Onyx vase
Materials: Vine, Spray mum

마른 素材 Dried Materials

마른 素材는 古木만이 아니고 여러가지 식물의 部分인 뿌리, 가지, 덩굴, 잎, 꽃, 열매 등을 말려서 쓰고 있다.

각기 다른 素材는 건조시키는 과정도 시기도 다르지만 계절에 따라 적절한 때에 적절한 처치를 해서 다양한 素材를 얻을 수 있다. 이 같은 素材들은 마른 後에 보여 주는 固有의 色相과 質感으로 살아 있는 素材에서 얻기 어려운 아름다움과 운치가 있어서 素材의 폭을 넓혀 주고 있다.

살아 있는 素材와 마른 素材의 配合은 서로를 더욱 돋보이게 한다. 즉 살아 있는 素材에 곁들여진 마른 素材는 한층 살아 있는 素材의 신선함을 강조한다. 반대로 마른 素材가 主役이 되고 살아있는 素材가 곁들여졌을 때는 마른 素材의 特色이 强調되고 対照的인 效果를 얻을 수가 있다. 또 古木, 마른 花草나 열매 뿐인 作品은 물을 쓰지 않는 利点이 있다.

추운 겨울날 花器의 물이 얼어 터져서 花器를 깰 念慮도 없고 構成이 자유로워서 空中에 달아 매거나 벽에 직접 걸어 놓을 수도 있고 花器의 바깥面이나 위에 혹은 거꾸로도 마음 먹은 대로 소화 시킬 수 있는 편리함이 있다. 그리고 무엇 보다도 오래 쓸 수 있다는 것이 마른 素材가 갖는 利点이다.

또 質感, 形態도 多様해서 해바라기 씨의 맷스(mass)状, 여러가지 잎의 面이나 山歸來의 재미있는 선과 점, 갈대의 부드러움 등등 近來에는 素材를 着色하거나 脱色하여 特殊한 色彩 效果를 올리고 있다.

많은 素材를 乾燥시킬 때에는 通風이 좋고 그늘진 場所에 거꾸로 매달아 서서히 말리는 것이 素材를 상하지 않게 하며 퇴색시키지 않는 건조 방법이다.

한번 사용한 素材나 마른 素材는 조심스럽게 종이에 싸서 어둡고 통풍이 잘 되는 곳에 보관하였다가 다시 사용 하도록 한다.

Intriguing dried materials can be created from a variety of sources: branches, roots, vines, leaves, flowers, berries and nuts. By taking advantage of what is available each season, a good supply can be kept on hand throughout the year. Dried materials offer colors and textures unobtainable in fresh plants, and their beauty will add a new dimension to your work.

In combination the dried and the fresh complement each other, the dried elements enhancing the vitality of the fresh material. If the major component of the arrangement is dried material, then the fresh material will emphasize its rough, stiff nature. At the same time, arrangements made of aged wood, dried grass and flowers, and berries are practical as they need no water. There is no danger in winter of water freezing and breaking a container, and the materials can be handled freely. They can be hung on a wall, arranged above the container or even upside-down. Best of all, dried materials keep well.

Opportunities for experimentation abound: the texture of a mass of sunflower seeds, the surfaces of various leaves, the sharp lines and staccato dots of green briar, the softness of pampas grass.

Although drying techniques differ somewhat from plant to plant, the simplest procedure is to hang the material upside-down in an airy, shady place, giving it plenty of time to dry thoroughly. In this way it will retain its color and is less likely to be damaged. After use, it should be wrapped carefully in paper and kept in a dark, well-ventilated place.

花器 작은 바구니
素材 판파스그라스, 데포딜, 호랑고비, 유채화

Container: Bamboo basket
Materials: Dried pampas grass, Dried mateuccia orientalis, Daffodil, Rape-blossom

観葉植物　Foliage Plants

観葉植物은 잎이 아름답고 글자 그대로 잎을 즐기는 植物을 말한다.

많은 사람들이 一年中 푸른 잎이 무성한 것 (熱帶植物이나 亞熱帶植物)으로 생각하기 쉽지만 樹木의 단풍진 아름다운 모습이라던가 옥잠화, 엽란같이 잎에 운치가 있는 것은 모두 観葉植物의 아름다움으로 손꼽힌다. 많이 쓰이는 아스파라거스는 代表的인 観葉植物이다.

素材로 쓰일 때 形態 質感 色彩에 따라 多様하게 쓰인다.

키가 큰 것, 面이 넓은 것, 잎의 모양에 특징이 있는 것, 부드러운 것, 딱딱한 것등 많은 종류가 있어 각기 특징이나 개성을 充分히 생각하여 꽃을 필요가 있다.

잎의 面은 보통 평평한 것이 많고 개 중에는 구부러진 面의 잎도 있다. 그리고 잎의 面은 平面的이라고 할 수 있다. 空間을 채우는 것이지만 平面的이기 때문에 量感이 없다. 面을 쌓아가서 立体的으로 하여 보다 힘이 주어지게 잎과 잎을 겹쳐서 쓰기도 한다. 또는 잎의 曲線을 바꾸어 구부러진 面을 과장해도 좋다.

여기서는 아스페레늄의 잎을 두장 교차 시켜 세우므로서 잎의 線을 여유있게 보이고 포피의 꽃잎의 부드러움이 아스페레늄 잎의 質感과 色調를 더욱 부각시켜 준다.

Arrangements based on foliage offer as much enjoyment as those that focus on flowers. Although it is commonly thought that the only foliage suitable for flower arrangements are the leaves of tropical plants that remain green thoughout the year, deciduous leaves also have great beauty as we can see in the vibrant colors of autumn leaves and the shape and curve of aspidistra and lily leaves. Another good example is asparagus, which is widely used for its foliage.

These materials can be arranged according to either their shape, their color, or their mood. One should also take advantage of their individual characteristics. Do they give a feeling of height or of volume? Do the leaves have an unusual shape? Are they supple or are they rigid?

Some leaves have a natural twist, but most are flat. These are employed as space fillers. Something has to be done, however, to give them volume. One way to achieve a solid impression is to combine many leaves. Bending and twisting the leaves to bring attention to their curvature is also helpful.

In the arrangement pictured here the natural shape and line of Japanese bird's nest have been enlivened by crossing them and contrasting them with the fragility of the poppy flowers.

花器　白磁花器
素材　아스페레늄, 포피 －
Container: White porcelain vase
Materials: Japanese birds-nest, Poppy

古木 Aged Wood

오랜 歲月 生命이 스쳐 간 古木은 素材로서 매우 貴重하다.

独特한 色彩와 形態 質感 등은 나무의 종류에 따라 다르고 뿌리와 가지의 부분에 따라서도 다르다.

오래동안 물에 잠겨 있다가 흘러 내려 온 流木은 또 다른 妙味가 있는 것이다.

写実的인 作品은 물론이고 非写実的인 表現을 할 때도 또 文人画的인 作品의 構成에도 폭넓게 쓸 수가 있다.

古木은 作品 속에서 重量感을 주기도 하고 여유 있는 空間構成에 도움이 되기도 하고 또 다른 素材를 고정시키는 便利한 存在이기도 하다.

Having grown through long years of exposure to wind and rain and sun, soon to reach the culmination of its life, an aged tree is a rare and precious material. Each tree has a unique color, form, and expression. The various parts of the tree, too, all display individual qualities.

Driftwood that has been submerged for a long time has a special character which lends itself to both naturalistic and abstract compositions, as well as the literati style. Versatile and useful, aged trees serve to give strength and majesty to an arrangement and to stabilize the other elements of the composition.

文人花 Literati Arrangement

文人이란 中国에서는 宋·明의 時代에, 韓国에서는 李朝時代에 学問이 있는 士大夫階級의 사람 가운데 文房(書齊)에서의 趣味的인 生活을 즐겨하던 사람들을 말한다.

이 文人들이 여가에 그린 그림을 文人画라고 하였다.

文人畵를 그리는데 있어서 畵題라 하여 그림으로 그리는 植物의 配合이 정해져 있다.

歲寒三友는 松竹梅를 말하고 四君子는 梅蘭菊竹을 이르는 말이다.

꽃의 선택이나 配合에 있어 높은 精神性과 詩情性이 요구되며 技術이 아니고 꽃는 사람의 교양이 나타나는 꽃이며 花材를 적게 쓰고 自然의 植物의 興趣를 살리면서 저마다의 꽃이 갖고 있는 德性까지도 사랑한다는 慣習이 있다.

東洋사람들이 追求하는 詩精神이 豊富한 文学性있는 高度의 表現이 要求되는 것이다.

The literati of what is known as the literati style were members of the leisured class of Sung Dynasty China and Yi Dynasty Korea who enjoyed a life of intellectual and artistic pursuits. Whenever they were not composing poems, they applied their brushes to ink paintings and their thoughts to flower arrangements. In the literati style of painting and flower arrangement, the number and combination of the plants in the composition strictly followed the principles of classical Chinese thought. Thus we have the "Three Friends of Winter"—pine, bamboo, and plum blossoms—and the "Four Gentlemen"—plum, orchid, chrysanthemum, and bamboo.

The choice of flowers and their composition demand delicately tuned aesthetic feelings, and greater value is placed on the person's sensibilities than on technique. Traditionally the materials are kept to a minimum in order to bring out the personality of the flowers, each one being cherished for itself. Filled with Oriental poetic feeling, the literati style asks the arranger to seek expression of a spiritual nature.

花器　白磁花瓶
素材　古木，牡丹
Container: White porcelain vase
Materials: Double peony, Moss-covered branch, Aged tree

花器　白磁花瓶
素材　소나무, 映山紅
Container: White porcelain
vase
Materials: Pine, Azalea

小品花　Small Arrangements

　한줄기의 가지를 어떻게 어떤 位置에서 보아야 가장 아름다운가는 素材의 形態를 보는 감각이 小品花를 꽂는 데 있어 중요한 일이다.

　華芸의 構成에 必要한 밸런스, 리듬, 움직임 볼륨 등의 原則을 충분히 공부할 必要가 있다.

　되도록 構成을 단순하게 素材의 아름다움을 自己의 美的 감각으로 追求하고 정리하는 것이 중요하다.

　한 가지라도 가장 아름답게 보이는 位置에서 다루지 않으면 전체적인 움직임 속에 調和를 얻기 어려우며 운치 있는 안정된 作品이 안 된다.

　Knowing how to place a branch to its best advantage is essential for small arrangements. The fundamentals of flower arrangement—balance, rhythm, movements, and volume —also must be mastered.

　Keep the composition as simple as possible and let your own feelings for the materials guide your expression. Unless each stem and branch is handled with sensitivity so that it appears at its most beautiful angle, the work will lack interest and harmony. Through its posture, viewing angle, and position each element works to complete the composition as a whole.

花器　白磁水盤
素材　洋蘭, 貝母꽃, 미리오그라다스아스파라거스

Container: White porcelain bowl
Materials: Dendrobium, Asparagus myriocladus, Fritillaria

花器　白磁小瓶
素材　나리, 수리취꽃

Container: White porcelain vase with
narrow mouth
Materials: Blue ball, Star lily

著者略歴　**Brief Personal History of the Author**

祖父代에 落郷하였던 江原道 平康에서 1924年 出生

小学校 5年 가을 서울에 帰京

華公이라는 이름은 今日의 그를 予知한 듯 祖父께서 지은 이름이다.

그는 李朝人의 生活 양식을 고수하고 열심히 꽃을 가꾸어 손님을 부르는 것을 楽으로 삼았다.

京畿公立高等女学校를 卒業한 가을부터 当時 서울에 滞留하던 日本 生花教授에게 師事한 바 있다.

2年 여의 修業은 짧은 期間이었지만 祖父와 더불어 그의 꽃의 生活에 커다란 영향을 미쳤다고 그녀는 말한다.

1958年은 韓国華芸에도 그녀에게도 意義있는 해였다.

第一回 任華公 華芸 小品展이 美国 公報院 (U. S. I. S.)에서 열리고 女性 月刊誌 女苑社가 定期華芸 講習会를 처음으로 始作한 해이기도 하다.

이는 戦後의 韓国 사람들은 물론 在留 外国人들에게도 크게 꽃으로 向한 마음을 넓혀주는 계기가 되기도 하였다.

1960年 第一回 会員展을 계기로 任華公꽃꽂이 同友会가 모아지고 1973年 社団法人 華公会로 改編되었다. 꽃으로 맺어진 内外 会員들은 1983年 12月 第41回 会員展을 열었다.

그간 国内個人展 6回와 日本을 비롯하여 米国 페루 等 여러나라에서 많은 展示会와 데몬스트레이션을 가진바 있다.

또한 미국 존슨 대통령을 비롯하여 国賓 방한시에도 데몬스트레이션이 행하여졌다.

現在 社団法人 華公会 理事長이고 서울 華公会館은 많은 会員의 研修 및 世界의 꽃친구들의 親善의 자리가 되고 있다.

서울 近郊 楊州에 있는 華公苑에는 그가 좋아하는 野生素材가 가꾸어져 있고 愛用하는 白磁花器도 완벽한 韓国伝統的 施設 아래 그녀 自身의 디자인으로 구어내고 있다.

Born in 1924 in Kang Won Do where her family had taken up temporary residence, Im Wha Kong was given her name meaning "Flower Companion" by her grandfather who foresaw in her an affinity with the beauty of flowers. One of the greatest influences in her life, her grandfather lived in the spirit of the Li Dynasty, enjoying the pleasure of good company and the cultivation of his garden.

After graduating from Kyeong-gi Girls' High School in Seoul, she began formal training in flower arrangement under a Japanese master living in Korea. These two years of intensive study marked the beginning of her life's devotion to the art of flowers.

In 1958 she held her first exhibition at U.S.I.S. (United States Information Service) and began teaching under the sponsorship of Nyeo Weon, Korea's leading women's monthly magazine. This was the first time that the Korean people had the opportunity to attend regularly held classes in flower arrangement.

In 1960 the Im Wha Kong Flower Arrangement Society was founded. This event was celebrated with an exhibition of works by its members, the first of many held under its auspices.

In 1973 the Society was incorporated as the Wha Kong Hoe. 1983 marked the 41st exhibition of the society whose membership by this time had reached far beyond the shores of Korea.

Besides the 6 private exhibitions she has held in the past two decades, Im Wha Kong is noted for her contribution to world friendship through the many demonstrations she has given abroad and for overseas visitors, notably on the occasion of the visit to Korea of Mrs. Lydon B. Johnson. Another achievement has been her popular program on flower arrangement on KBS, the national television network.

Presently she is the chair of the Wha Kong Hoe. Its school in Seoul offers lessons in flower arrangement and acts as a meeting place for people who love flowers the world over.

Near Seoul she has established a botanical garden where she cultivates wild plants she has carefully collected. Here, too, is a kiln where white porcelain vases of her own design are produced according to traditional techniques.